THE Shepherd
THE Sheep
&
THE Sheepdog

A Call to Order
Within the Body of Christ

ANGELA D. OLIPHANT
FOREWORD BY KARIN RAWLS

Copyright © 2016 Angela D. Oliphant

All rights reserved.

ISBN-13: 978-1-954818-08-8

Studio Griffin
A Publishing Company
Garner, North Carolina
www.studiogriffin.net

The Shepherd, The Sheep and The Sheepdog:
A Call to Order Within the Body of Christ
Copyright © 2016 Angela D. Oliphant
All Rights Reserved

Cover Design by Ruth E. Griffin
Image by Orientaly/Shutterstock

Scripture quotations taken from The King James Version (Public Domain).

This book is licensed for your personal enjoyment only and may not be reproduced, transmitted or stored in whole or in part by any means including graphic, electronic or mechanical without expressed written consent of the author.

Blog: livingonpurpose139.wordpress.com
Email: livingonpurpose31@gmail.com
Facebook: facebook.com/Whole-Beautiful-168375196636890/?fref=ts

Printed in U.S.A

Acknowledgement

A big THANK YOU to my heavenly Father who is the ultimate true Shepherd. You have loved me with an everlasting love and given me the wisdom written on each page of this book.

To each and every family member and friend that helped me and encouraged me along the way. I am forever grateful.

A special and heartfelt thank you to my publisher Studio Griffin who brought this dream into reality!

I love and appreciate you all!

Foreword

I want to congratulate my friend of over two decades, Angela Oliphant, on the accomplishment of her first book THE SHEPHERD, THE SHEEP AND THE SHEEP DOG. This book was birthed out of the love for the Father, His dealings, purpose, will, and plan for His beloved children. The Shepherd, The Sheep, and The Sheep Dog are familiar subject matters of the Bible, yet we often miss, and misunderstand their application because of our cultural differences. Minister Angela is revealing these divine secrets that are irrevocably bound up with the basic subjects in an easy to understand way, through stories, applications, and insight given by the One who gave them. This book will give you a spiritual vesting to execute God's purpose on the earth. Open your heart to relevant, new truths of God's care and divine order. As you turn each page, receive a spiritual deposit that will work as a seed that will bring for much lasting fruit.

Radical for Him,
Karin Rawls

CONTENTS

Preface	1
Introduction	3
Chapter 1: Order	9
Chapter 2: The Shepherd	17
Chapter 3: The Relationship with the Sheep	24
Chapter 4: Sheepherders, The Support	31
Chapter 5: The Sheep	39
Chapter 6: Sheep Under Attack	45
Chapter 7: Productivity of Sheep	53
Chapter 8: Caring for the Sheep	59
Conclusion	65
Prophetic Prayer for Order	71
About the Author	75

THE Shepherd THE Sheep & THE Sheepdog

Angela D. Oliphant

Preface

When we take the time to study the earth, vegetation, animals, etc., we begin to see the Kingdom of God and how it operates. There is an order in which things operate and without that order, there would be no progression; things would be at a standstill and would cease to live.

Many years ago, before I thought about writing this book, before I even thought about order, I was at the library, searching for a good book to read. I came across one about sheep and shepherds. This peaked my interest because I had been studying sheep in the word of God so I thought maybe this book about natural sheep would help me better understand "spiritual sheep" and their shepherds. As I delved into the book, I was amazed to find out why our heavenly Father references those who are His to sheep and why so many leaders in the Bible were shepherds that tended to sheep before they tended to people.

As you began reading the pages of this book, please understand, I am not a scholar on the subject nor do I profess to be. This is just a simple study I've done with the guidance and wisdom of the Holy Spirit. My prayer and my intent is to relay revelation and information that will inspire you to study more and learn something that can be applied to your everyday life.

Introduction

There is a blessing that comes upon the local church and the body of Christ as a whole when we are obedient and heed the call to order. Often times in ministry people "feel" as though they can do what they want, say what they want, and live the way they want; but according to scripture there is a way we should live, speak, and conduct our lives.

If you observe the earth and how it functions, it works according to order. The moon doesn't fight the sun for its position during the day; nor does the sun fight the moon for the night. The moon "knows" it is the light for the night and it does its job well. It realizes the light it has is lesser than the brightness of the sun and is perfectly fine with that. Each works within the capacity it has been assigned.

When reading the book of Genesis, the first book of the Bible, we see how everything was given a place and time to come forth. The waters were told how far they could come and even though at one point they covered the earth, God spoke to them to recede and allow dry land to come forth. The waters didn't "fight" against God, they listened and withdrew, allowing the land to come forth. All throughout antiquity and the history of the word of God, the Blessing always came when there was order.

Martin Luther King, Jr. was a man of order and he taught others how to walk in that same order. When persecution came, he showed others how they could remain men and women of dignity and not falter. Just because others were angry and hurting each other didn't mean the same reaction should come from those who were under attack. Due to Mr. King's order and organized efforts, a change was made in the earth that is still evolving today.

* * *

Let's look at the word 'order'. Webster's dictionary defines order as a condition where there is logical agreement of the disposition of things; sequence or succession; method; an instruction for a person to follow; to command; to demand. Method is an orderly arrangement, a process or the regular way of doing something. Instruction is the act of teaching important knowledge and lessons that give direction. Order only works if it is followed; it is a matter of the heart and obedience. A business, a family, a church, and even a world without order means no productivity or moving forward. All these areas could not function without order; they would just exist in a continued circular motion, never attaining, achieving or accomplishing anything.

On my quest to seek out order and how it could cause blessings to be upon me, my family, and my local church, I felt prompted in my spirit to take a look at sheep. Sheep always follow order and never fight against authority. They need the leadership of their shepherd in order to survive – indeed, depending on the shepherd is the only way they get to their next destination or even their next meal. Sheep stay in one place and never go anywhere to find more food or take in different scenery. They are content in the place they are in and need the nudging and leadership of the shepherd so they can move forward and prosper.

Many who are reading these words right now are probably saying, "Well, God, I am not a sheep. I can think for myself and do for myself, I don't need to depend on anyone else." There is some truth to this statement because God has given us a brain to think and go far beyond the thoughts of a sheep, but in His word, he tells us that we are His sheep, and he is our Shepherd. Though we may have our own thought processes and can think for ourselves, the Father wants us to willingly lay it all down for His direction and His thought process, so we can receive instruction - this important knowledge that will become wisdom unto us and give us much needed direction that causes us to prosper and be blessed beyond measure!

In the pages of this book, I plan to take you on a journey and show you the wonder of having order in your life, your family, your business and your local church. It will be awesome to see the transformation in your life once this nugget of wisdom has been applied to your life. Don't let these words merely fall on "deaf" ears and hardened hearts. Ask the Holy Spirit to speak to you and breathe His revelatory winds upon your spirit man so you can not only hear but receive what he is speaking to you.

Angela D. Oliphant

Chapter 1:
Order

Order seems to be such a rare thing in today's world of social media and what people now deem as their freedom of speech and right to do whatever they choose. Times have indeed changed - some changes have been for the better while others have not been so beneficial. Social graces were, at one point in history, the norm for everyone and it was rare to see someone act out of order and be disrespectful to others. They may have been upset and thought things but those statements were voiced in the privacy of their own homes or amongst those whom they saw as close friends.

If we would take the opportunity to observe and look in depth into successful businesses, organizations, etc., we see that order is one of the main reasons for the success of these former eras. Anything that is always in chaos is not prospering nor is it going to prosper. 'Chaos', according to Webster's Dictionary, is *complete confusion and disorder: a state in which behavior and events are not controlled by anything.* But when we look at the Bible, we see how everything was called forth and put into order. In the beginning, the earth was without form; it had no boundaries, everything was intermingled together. All components were there to bring forth something awesome and great but needed to be put in some kind of order. Once order was established, we saw the Sun, Moon, Stars, trees, grass, animals of all kinds, waters, seas, oceans, and the list goes on and on. None of these things would have been seen, noticed, or enjoyed if they were not given the opportunity to "shine" through the voice of order. When God spoke order into the earth, it was then able to bring forth all its wonder and amazement for all to see.

Every person, organization and business has the potential of being something wonderful or someone great and awesome but it all depends on that person or entity answering the "call" to order. When order is a part of the equation, prosperity and peace are sure to follow. We should seek after order like we would buried treasure. It is worth more than all the money in the world. Without order, your body couldn't function, finances would be in disarray, and life itself would not be as we know it today.

Think about your automobile: it may have a nice paint job, tires, and rims but if things are not in order under the hood, if the engine has parts that have been misplaced, if the battery has been put on the seat beside you and not in its proper place, the car would not be able to work. You can have all the parts to the car and have them all laid out in a garage but if they are not put together in their correct places in the order they were made to function, you will never get the ultimate use out of your vehicle. Now you may be able to take something out of place and the vehicle will continue to work but it will not work at its full potential because some things have been moved out of their assigned order.

A similar analogy can be used with the human body; it has many members and each member has a place of operation and order so that it can function properly. The eyes don't try to smell and the ears don't attempt to see. Each part has a specific function that operates in the order it was given.

The Bible states that believers are a body fitly joined together with each joint supplying what the other needs (Ephesians 4:16). To be fitly joined together means there is order. Each joint is in its proper place and it is giving the other joints what they need to continue to prosper.

In Ephesians chapter 6, the Bible speaks of the armor that we are to wear as Christians. This armor is an armor of order; each part of the armor is specifically made for a specific part of the body and by following the order and wearing it properly, you can excel and move forward, but if worn out of order and not on the right body part, you could lose the battle or get harmed in the process. David knew this when Saul wanted to give him his armor to fight the Philistine Goliath (I Samuel 17:38-39). David understood Saul's armor was not the "order" for Him - he had to utilize the "armor" God had given him. By doing so, he defeated Goliath with a sling shot and stones; and while this order worked for David, it probably would not have worked for

Saul. The lesson here is that order is much needed and cannot be thrown away, laid to the side or forgotten.

The God we serve is a God of order and we must be a people of order if we say we have accepted Christ in our hearts. All throughout the Bible we are given instruction on how things should take place. From how to be born again, to how to live, how to stand in the midst of trouble and strife; and what it takes to prosper and be in good health. All these things have a certain order that must be adhered to, else it will not work.

A baby is not born full grown. It is first a seed planted in its mother's womb where it takes nine months for this baby to grow and develop so it can come forth into the world. Even when the baby arrives, he or she doesn't come into the earth speaking eloquently and eating steak and potatoes. This child has to follow the order of growth and development; the order that has been put into place in the earth for him. When Jesus was given the assignment to come into the earth; He did so according to the order the Father had put in place.

He couldn't come into the earth fully grown; he had to come as a babe and grow and mature into a man.

Now, since God himself follows order, how can those who say they follow him feel like they are exempt from it? That they somehow have special privileges that exclude them from being a people of order? We must understand order has nothing to do with feelings. You may not "feel" like following order but when you do, the Blessing will come upon you. Notice I didn't say blessings but *the* Blessing. What is meant by the Blessing is the everlasting honor and "stamp" of approval from the Father. This Blessing comes upon you and never leaves as long as you have aligned yourself with the word of God and have chosen to be a person of order. Just knowing that you have God's approval and favor forever should have you seeking out what you have to do to get your life in order.

Order is hard work and takes discipline but the benefits far outweigh what it takes to attain it. When you are living the life of order, you are not going to be perfect and without flaw but you will be in a place where God's grace and mercy abounds in your life; a place where His love covers you on all sides; a place where you know you can come to the Father boldly knowing that he hears you and answers every cry, call and prayer.

Through the remaining chapters in this book, I will share with you the order of the Shepherd and his Sheep. We will look at this from natural and spiritual points of view. You will also discover why the Father compares us to sheep; why He is said to be the Shepherd, and why He has appointed apostles, pastors, teachers, prophets and evangelists in the body of Christ. I am sure you will be amazed and inspired; which in turn will provoke you to change and align yourself with God's word. As the scriptures say, all this is indeed for the perfecting of the saints until we all come into maturity. It's time to grow up, trust God and live the life he has called you to. This day, order has come to your house!

Angela D. Oliphant

Chapter 2:
The Shepherd

A shepherd is a person who leads, guides and takes care of sheep. One definition says a shepherd is a pastor. They are not babysitters who are there to temporarily watch a child; they have the awesome responsibility of being good parents who take care of their children. Good Shepherds take care of their sheep, unlike the shepherds in Ezekiel 34:16.

> *I will seek that which was lost, and bring again that which was driven away, and will bind up that which was broken, and will strengthen that which was sick: but I will destroy the fat and the strong; I will feed them with judgment.*

In this verse, the Bible speaks of men who are not true shepherds. It shows us what they did which is out of character of being a shepherd. And as I looked at what a shepherd shouldn't be doing, I began to see what he should do. Simply, the negatives could be positives if God's principles were obeyed instead of dismissed. When the latter occurs, the sheep (spiritual sheep) hurt, become wounded, abused, to the point of death. Let's take a look at these shepherds and what could have been done to bring order back to their lives and those they should have been taking care of.

The word of God says that the shepherds were more concerned with feeding themselves than feeding the sheep. To turn this whole situation around, the shepherds needed to start caring for the sheep and feeding them the sincere milk of the word of God. Shepherds should be teaching the word and laying a foundation of truth in their sheep. Leading them to areas where there are lush, healthy fields of "grass", places where they will not be poisoned with weeds that will cause sickness and disease to come upon them. Shepherds should always have a good word, a productive and life changing word to sow into their sheep. Not giving them leftovers from someone else's message or prayers - stealing from someone else's fields to feed their own. They should spend time in the presence of the Father and get his direction for the sheep he has assigned to them.

The shepherd needs to build up his sheep, not tear them down. Yes, sheep need to be corrected but they don't need to be beat upon and left to die. As the ultimate Shepherd, Father God chastises us but he always does it in love. He doesn't beat sheep just because he can; he causes us to feel saddened or embarrassed by our actions; he prunes, purifies and refines us. The chastening he brings causes his sheep to grow, not throw in the towel, give up and quit.

Shepherds should declare healing into the lives of their sheep - emotional, social, physical, financial healing. They should desire to see healing come forth everywhere their sheep display hurt. They should "doctor" the injured and attend to them until they know their injuries are being healed from the inside out. It should never be a burden for a shepherd to labor with a sheep; deep wounds may take longer but it is well worth the prayers, declaration and love spent.

Shepherds need to start going after those sheep that have strayed away. They should never let their heart get so hard that they can look at a lost sheep and say "good riddance", "goodbye" and "don't let the doorknob hit ya'". They should never be comfortable with a sheep leaving. There should be a hurting, a concern, a love instead, that would say "come back into the fold", a heart that desires to see that the sheep is revived and restored.

In essence what every shepherd needed in Ezekiel 34 was a heart change. The same can be said of shepherds in todays' church. Their hearts need to be like the heart of God; not selfish and self-serving. As you read further in this scripture we see God declare that he himself will go look for those sheep that have gone astray. He would rescue them, bring them back to the fold and feed them. This speaks volumes about the heart of those who were out of order as shepherds. They were going against the heart of God, more content with serving themselves than serving their sheep.

When there is no order in "the head" (leadership) the whole "body" suffers. To bring this into perspective, look at yourself and your physical body. If your head hurts, it affects your entire body simply because something is out of order. Your whole body wants to cater to the fact that your head is hurting. Although you may still be able to function and get things done; it doesn't mean the pain has left your head. How many churches in today's society continue to function with disorder in the head? These churches are dysfunctional, and spiritually, they are dying; and the sad thing is most of them don't even know it.

Shepherds who have lost sight of their way trust in their own insight instead of following Jesus and what he placed as guidelines for them to follow. In Psalm 23 we read:

The Lord is my Shepherd - I shall not want.

Another translation states:

Because the Lord is my Shepherd; I have everything I need.

This first line says it all. A shepherd should have everything that his sheep need. Whatever guidance, comfort, love, direction or care the sheep requires, the shepherd should be able to provide. Likewise, the ultimate desire of a shepherd's heart should be to help their sheep prosper and grow.

The shepherd has been given the awesome delegated authority from the chief Shepherd to attend to his sheep; to love and care for them as He would. To walk successfully in this delegated authority shepherds must know the heart of the Father and have the desire to follow him. Webster's dictionary defines the heart is the principle organ that causes blood to circulate in the body. This organ is regarded as the seat of vitality, intellect and emotion (love, kindness, pity), courage, determination, enthusiasm; the inner, central or essential part.

The Chief Shepherd causes his blood to flow and circulate, bringing healing, salvation, deliverance and freedom. He is the seat of our vitality which is the power to live - the very power of life itself! He is and directs every emotion we may have. He is love, kindness, pity, courage, determination and enthusiasm in our lives. He is the inner, central and essential part of who we are. He is the Chief

Shepherd and he requires this kind of heart to reside in all of his shepherds.

True shepherds of the Most High must arise and come forward during this time when faith itself is on trial and people are turning away from church and God. They need to go after the lost and love on them, care for them, and bring them home. They don't need to beat them, bash them, and push them further away. Sheep should have a healthy respect for their shepherd and should never be ashamed or fearful of them. They should know that whenever they are in the presence of their shepherd, they are safe. They should never feel like they are in danger when their shepherd is around.

In today's society, some shepherds try to "crossover" into roles they were never "called" or "chosen" to do. They believe pastoring their local church is not profitable for them. Instead, they feel the need to travel and minister all over the world and not grow their congregation up in the word. To be profitable means yielding advantageous returns or results; it has absolutely nothing to do with money. It is about returns and results that are favorable. These returns and results are not only for the pastor but also for the sheep; showing each favor in the eyes of God and man. It is a two-way relationship: shepherds should do their part and the sheep should also do their part. In the case of the shepherd, he is the heart of the church. He / she keeps the blood pumping throughout the ministry; feeling what the ministry goes through and knowing how to lead and guide them to better pastures. Shepherds should never leave their pastor-ship to walk in an office they were never called to; they should never attempt to "walk out" the whole five-fold ministry. They must realize the power they have as being a pastor will not operate in the office of an evangelist, teacher, prophet or apostle. The anointing to be a pastor is just that: the anointing to pastor! Moving outside of that calling and trying to be all things to all people will put you in a state of unrest, of being unfulfilled and lost.

Shepherds, operate where you are graced to.

Chapter 3:
The Relationship with the Sheep

Once a person has accepted Christ as their savior, they become His sheep – spiritually. Now they have to start "eating" properly to grow their spirit, which at this point is like a new born baby - a baby who is dependent upon the Shepherd to feed, teach, lead, guide, correct, encourage and love them. The objective for the Shepherd is to help sheep grow up and become who God has desired them to be before the beginning of time. But a lot of "sheep" live beneath where they have been called to be.

The Shepherd's purpose is to cause the spirit of the sheep to live and thrive so that their "flesh" (wrong attitudes, lifestyles and thoughts) starve and die! As a parent would help their newborn baby so a shepherd should help his sheep. When they are babies, treat them like babies. Handle them with much care and love. Feed, change, cuddle and play with them so that they can get plenty of rest and grow. And as they grow, they learn what is right and what is wrong; what will hurt and what's okay. They start to move around a little bit, they crawl. At this stage, they have to be watched more because now they are getting into things that at one time was out of reach. They have no discerning of good and evil so they need the shepherd's guidance and leadership.

A shepherd needs to be able to know his sheep in order to be an effective leader. He / she needs to be able to minister to each and every sheep who has been assigned to them. Realization of where their sheep are spiritually is a must. The sheep can't be treated like a newborn when they are toddlers and toddlers can't be treated like teenagers. A shepherd can't expect a maturity level to come forth out of the newly saved person like they would with someone who has been saved for twenty years, while sometimes you have sheep who may mature early. Shepherds should always know their sheep and where they "stand" so they can better assist them in their walk with Christ.

Every shepherd should be able to handle and manage the sheep they have with love and not manipulation and control. How else could you leave the ninety-nine to go after the one (Matthew 99:12) when you don't even know you have ninety-nine or that one is missing? A shepherd has to be personable and available but still maintain his/her authority with integrity.

The shepherd and the sheep's relationship should be one that is valued by both parties. The sheep should appreciate, honor and respect the shepherd and vice versa. Although the shepherd is the authority figure over the sheep, he or she should still have a love for their sheep that causes the sheep to know they are safe and that they are celebrated. No matter what stage or age they are, sheep need to know that the shepherd is not just "putting up" with them. The word of God tells us that by this shall all men know that we are His disciples; if we have love one for another (John 13:35).

Love has a bond that cannot be broken or destroyed when it is pure. Whether we are walking in the role of a shepherd or a sheep, our prayer should be:

Lord let your love overtake me and shine through to all people, even if no one remembers my name or my accomplishments in life, let them remember the love they felt coming from my heart to theirs; from my spirit to theirs. Let them remember that whenever they were in my presence, they felt loved and appreciated.

Love will always cause a person to "grow" - to move forward and accomplish great feats! When an individual knows they are loved, it enables them to reach for what would have been the unreachable at one time. It will permit them to press through hardness and heartache and come out of it rejoicing, all the while gaining momentum. Love is what motivates a shepherd to go after the one as well as be in tune with the ninety-nine. And it is what prompts the sheep to follow after the shepherd with no inhibitions, trusting him every step of the way.

The relationship between the Shepherd and sheep is awesome to experience, naturally and spiritually.

Much time and effort is involved but it is always worth it.

Angela D. Oliphant

Chapter 4:
Sheepherders, The Support

In the natural, sheepherders are sheep dogs trained to keep the sheep "in line" and following the direction of the shepherd. If a sheep gets away from the flock, the sheep dog barks and corrals it back to the fold.

Sheepherders can never "hang out" with or around the sheep; nor spend a lot of downtime with them. If this happens, the sheep will begin to see the sheepherder as one of them and will not listen when the sheepherder attempts to save them or get them back in line with the shepherd. Even when the sheep sleep, the sheepherder / sheepdog sleep in a separate place.

I was excited when I first learned this information because I now understood why leaders should not hang out with the members of their congregation and why those whom they have appointed as leaders should never fraternize with the sheep either. This is not to say that leaders shouldn't show them kindness and love; it simply means there is an order that has to be followed. Like the parent / child or adult / child relationship, parents may have an awesome relationship with their children but they should never be on the same level as their child. The latter should always understand that even though their parents are "cool" and can talk and do things with them, they will never be at a point where they are equal with them. Sheep need to realize that they are loved even if they are not buddies or pals with the leaders and /or pastors of their local church.

There are boundaries that should never be crossed and this applies not only to the one who leads or supports the leaders but also for those who are following. In today's society, people want to believe they are all equal and have the same gifts. No matter what a person can do, we can do it too and do it better. However, this is not true; we were created with a divine and unique purpose; and if it's not embraced and nurtured, the world will never see or know what could have been. We, as sheep and as sons and daughters in the body of Christ, must realize that we are at our best when we are living the life the Father has designed for us and operating in the awesome gifts he has given each and every one of us.

And he gave some, apostles; and some, prophets; and some, evangelists; and some, pastors and teachers (Ephesians 4:11). It does not say he gave all but some - no one person can do it all. God put us together and gave us all different things to do because it was pleasing in his sight. He loves to see all the differences come together and make something beautiful. Not competing but complimenting. Look at nature: the trees don't compete with the flowers nor do the flowers compete with the grass or the grass try to "out shine" the soil; they all complement each other and together create an awesome picture for us to enjoy. The sun and the moon both give us light but neither tries to take the other's place.

Sheep need to get in place and love being sheep! Sheepherders / sheepdogs need to get in place and be the best at what they do. The sheepherder can't be the shepherd and the shepherd can't be the sheepherder. Each of them have duties that need to be performed or nothing will get accomplished. Flourish where you are planted: the ground where God has placed you is fertile and you can thrive there. Ultimately, the choice to do so is yours.

Ask yourself these questions: what is hindering me from being who God has made me to be? Why am I struggling with being a sheep? Why do I think that I have to work twice as hard to measure up to others who have a different rank or title? Why am I competing with those whom I should be complementing? Why am I feeling intimidated or inadequate?

These questions should prompt you to do a self-study: as children of the Most High, we should always hold fast to the word of God and know who we are by the Spirit, even if we don't "feel" like it in our flesh. Flesh should never be the defining factor!

Likewise, as a shepherds/pastor, you are only as good as your support. You can't be a phenomenal pastor and have a "weak" support team. You should surround yourself with people who are confident in their relationship with Christ and are not intimidated by you or any other leader. These people are not arrogant and vulgar but they know who they are and whom they belong to. Their primary goal is to please the Father. Embracing people who are strong in the Lord and have "His" heart and agenda will only benefit the pastor and the congregation. Some people who deem themselves to be pastors are only people who are manipulators and want to be in control. They don't have the Father's heart; just their own agenda. God is not consulted about anything. Everything is for and about them.

When appointing those who will be the support (the sheepherders), a shepherd must hear from the Ultimate Shepherd. Even when Jesus lived here on this earth he did not haphazardly choose those who would be his disciples. He made his decision by discernment and guidance from the Father; and selected the men who would become the disciples. And with these twelve came a change that affected them and the lives of those whom they came in contact with. Did they do everything right? No, but they had the heart and the character needed for the task at hand. No one said they had to be perfect but they had to be the ones the Father approved of. These were the twelve for the job.

Shepherds, choose the ones that the Father has chosen! Will they all have the same characteristics? No. Will they all do everything by the Bible and never make mistakes, no. Is it possible that at times they may overreact? Yes. Will there be one who may betray you? Yes. Will there be one who will deny they even know who you are when trouble arises? Yes. Regardless of this though, you must choose whom the Father has already chosen because as a pastor will realize and know that these things have to take place in order for scriptures to be fulfilled. When pastors truly grasp this, their lives will be more free and uninhibited. Even with all their issues, these disciples were not thorns or stumbling blocks to Jesus' ministry; each of them was a piece of the prophecy that had to be fulfilled, so that his life could be completed. Without them, the story of Jesus would have been altered and the ultimate goal would have never been reached.

Pastors, you need to support those whom you have appointed to be your sheepherders. They support you but the same support needs to be reciprocated. Trust and know that decisions made with the assistance of the Holy Ghost are the Father's decisions and he is always right in what he does. The only decision you should question is the one you've made without seeking the guidance of the Father.

This is why sheepherders are a necessity. As the shepherd focuses on the Ultimate Shepherd, the sheep need to focus on the shepherd and the way he/she is going. So the sheepherder focuses on the sheep: are they straying away? Are they hurt or wounded? Are they going in the right direction? Sometimes we have it all backwards: we think that it's the shepherd's job to do this. We need only to go back to scripture to see Jesus' focus was the Father and the mission that was set before him, while the disciples cared for the people (sheep). Jesus taught and trained his disciples continually but it was only on occasion that the people were gathered together while he ministered to them. Even when the multitudes assembled to listen to Jesus teach, he made the disciples responsible for feeding them. He blessed what they had available, but they were the ones who fed the people (Matthew 14:19).

As stated earlier, we must step into the call we have been ordained for, so that we can be the most effective. We may be doing great things but awesome things start to happen when we operate in our God-given call.

Chapter 5: The Sheep

Some see sheep as the dumbest and lowest of all animals, but they are smarter than most of their counterparts and just as productive and valuable. And in this chapter, we will see just how important sheep are. Hopefully you'll find a new understanding of sheep that will cause you to love and appreciate not just those who lead but also those who follow.

When Jesus lived and walked upon this earth, he was "limited" to whom he could minister to and touch, but once he died, the whole world opened up to him. He could touch far more people through His death, burial and resurrection. A similar thing happens with sheep. They have so great a heart to follow their leader, it shows through the way they live and die.

First of all, let's look at the definition of a sheep so we can have a foundation on which to build. A sheep is an animal related to the goat, raised for its meat, coat and skin. Though similar in stature, one of the major differences between the goat and the sheep is their covering. The sheep has a thick wooly covering and the goat's covering is long or short thin hair. We could say that the sheep have a better "covering" than the goat; which is true physically and spiritually.

Sheep are herding animals which means they live together in groups and are gregarious: they love to be in the company of others. They will not purposely walk away from the herd to be alone. If they are separated from the herd, they were either pulled away by a predator or they inadvertently wandered away. This is why the Shepherd will leave the ninety-nine to go after the one because the Shepherd knows his sheep would not leave under "normal" circumstances.

One of the first things people notice about sheep is their wooly coats, their covering. Sheep are sheered so the wool can be utilized to make coats, sweaters, hats and so much more. Their wool is sought after and is a very lucrative commodity. As we look naturally at the wooly coat of the sheep, we can compare it the spiritual covering that spiritual sheep have as individuals - prayer. Prayer is a covering that works in all types of circumstances and situations. Sheep should cover other sheep in prayer continuously.

Sheep skin is also a hot commodity. Both the wool and the skin are sought after and bring in a lot of money. And while the wool is given while the sheep is alive, the skin is offered in death. Sheep should be as Jesus: they should have the heart to not only "take a yearly trip" to the shearing building but if needed they would be willing to lay down their very lives for the other sheep. This happens in intercession where you literally take on the pressures and burdens of another and carry them because the others are not able to bear them. The wool is a prayer relationship; the skin is intercession – a deeper, more intimate level of prayer.

Sheep's meat is also a quality product: it is considered a delicacy; which means it's costly to purchase, just as it cost Jesus a high price to "purchase" us so that we could live for Him freely. He laid down his life so that we could live! Through Jesus' death, he could touch more, heal more and travel to more places to minister, because the limitations of his physical body were removed. So with sheep: through their deaths (their unselfish hearts and lives), they can feed more, clothe more and provide more. We as sheep have got to learn to "die"; for it's in our "death" that lives are changed, people are healed and our Father is glorified!

Sheep in their death can be utilized for glue. In the natural, glue puts things back together; it attaches one object to another. In the spiritual, this glue-like ability is the supernatural ability to walk in unity one with another. It means I will not allow any outside or inside force to separate me from my brothers or sisters in the faith. No matter what happens or what comes about, I will stick with them till the end.

A substance called tallow also comes from sheep. It is melted down fat used to make candles and soap. These two things are very significant in our Christian walk: candles provide light, while soap gives us cleanliness. Both offer us fragrance. We as sheep need to be a sweet-smelling aroma unto the Father through our everyday lives and personal walk with him. Our light needs to be in a place where all can see and be drawn to Jesus, while our lives need to be cleaned by the "washing" of the word of the Lord. We should be as white as snow; or should I say as white as sheep's wool.

In some instances, sheep are used as fertilizer. Fertilizer enhances the soil in which seeds are planted; it helps the seeds grow and flourish. Spiritual sheep should have this effect on each other. They need to walk as encouragers in the faith, speaking life into and causing each other to progress forward, spiritually and physically. Growth should always be a part of our relationships with each other. The word of God says that iron sharpens iron! Our lives should be about complimenting one another, not competing or killing each other.

Another product we get from sheep is cosmetics. These are utilized to enhance our appearance and create skin that is healthy and clean. Cosmetics cover us just like the love of God does! Love doesn't expose, it deals with you so that permanent changes can be made. It also shines through brighter from those of us who are walking and living the love walk.

One last thing that sheep are utilized for that I would like to share with you, the reader, is catgut. Catgut is a type of cord prepared from the natural fiber found in the walls of sheep intestines. These cords are used to string up tennis rackets. This spoke volumes to me, because tennis racket strings have to be pulled extremely tight in order to do their job. If they are loose, the racket is worthless. Spiritually speaking, sheep have to be able to be stretched beyond their limits and hold up under pressure. When a "ball" is hit in our direction, we should have enough strength and stamina to hit the ball back, having the confidence that in the end there is victory!

With all things, there is a good side and bad side. Sheep can be productive but they also can be attacked by harmful bugs and insects that will reverse their output. In the next few pages, we will discuss the things that distract and kill the sheep if they are not alert to their surroundings: paying attention to themselves, each other and the Shepherd they are following.

Angela D. Oliphant

Chapter 6:
Sheep Under Attack

Just as every part of the sheep is productive; every part can be attacked. As we look at a few parts of the sheep that get attacked and what damage can occur, think about yourself and ask the Father to reveal any attacks you may be experiencing in your life. Identifying the attacks will help you receive your deliverance and give you a way of escape. It may even give you the insight so these attacks will not be able to come upon you unaware. Knowledge is powerful; and when you comprehend the attack of the enemy and recognize your own failings, you will understand how to live a better, more purposeful life.

The first attack on the sheep we will discuss is the bot fly, which is any of a variety of stout, two-winged flies whose larvae are parasitic. The botfly lives off the sheep, penetrating the nasal passages and sinus cavities causing the sheep to lose its sense of smell. Notice how the botfly isn't seen; it's not out in the open to be easily detected; it's hidden, affecting the sheep over time.

Spiritually, this happens to sheep that start to lose their ability to discern. At one time, they viewed certain things as sin, but now it's ok. At one point, they guarded their hearts and were careful about what they allowed in, however, now they seem not to care. The enemy is very subtle, cleverly hiding things within others to make you think nothing is wrong. Even though sheep follow their shepherd, they have to be keen in their discernment. Nothing should come or show up in their lives without them being aware of what is going on.

The second attack on sheep comes in the form of mosquitoes. They land on you to suck your blood, to suck your very life! Some people have horrible reactions to mosquito bites while others just swat them and move on. Regardless, they are aggravating and can be harmful to the point of death. For the sheep, mosquitoes mainly attack their ears; which affects their ability to hear. When attacked in the same way, spiritual sheep are unable to hear the Shepherd when he calls for them or when he gives them instruction. Mosquitoes have a high pitch "buzz" that along with the biting cause a major distraction. This is another tactic the enemy uses to keep "spiritual sheep" off track. The word of God tells us that man shall not live by bread alone but by every word that proceeds from the Father's mouth (Matthew 4:4). So how can you hear when your ears are under attack? By being watchful and careful about what we listen to and hear. Some say the eyes are the window to our soul and that may very well true; I believe the ears are an opening to our spirit and we have to guard what we allow in our ears and eyes. The more you hear and accept the truth of the word of God, the less you listen and are influenced by the lies of the devil.

The third and final attack we will discuss is the blowfly. These flies cannot be controlled, they are everywhere. The only way a shepherd can help is to keep all exposed skin of the sheep clean and avoid injuries. If the sheep is wounded, it must be treated promptly! Otherwise where there are festering sores, injured skin, even where skin is folded over, blowflies can lay eggs and cause the sheep to die a slow death. And the thing about it is the injury doesn't have to be "new" - it can be one that has been there awhile.

We as spiritual sheep need to deal with things quickly to keep our spirit man "clean". We cannot allow things to stay and fester because those that rankle will cause our spirits to die, while our bodies contend with sickness. You can't get rid of the fly so you must get rid of what's attracting the fly! Since exposed skin lures the fly, you need to be covered then. You must be under a covering ordained by God: pastors/shepherds who have the heart of God. Deal with your issues, hurts, pains and disappointments quickly. Don't allow anything that may inflict harm on you to linger. These things are not worth your life! Face them and move on.

One last thing that stuck out to me is that the flies will lay eggs in skinfolds; which happens when a person is overweight or have lost a lot of weight. If they have skin folds, they can also have sores and wounds. Sometimes we take on too much and carry burdens we were never meant to carry. We need to cast all our cares upon the Lord and allow Him to take full control. Even when those things have been released, we must deal with whatever aftermath is left. We should love our lives to the point of doing whatever it takes to live fully and fulfill our purpose in the earth. Don't die "burdened by association". Leave the baggage you were never meant to carry.

Angela D. Oliphant

Chapter 7:
Productivity of Sheep

Based on what we discussed, we can surmise sheep are more productive in death than they are in life.

> *John 12:24 Verily, Verily I say unto to you, except a corn of wheat fall into the ground and die, it abideth alone: but if it die, it bringeth forth much fruit.*

There are four areas concerning sheep's productivity: three of them result from the sheep giving his life while only one can be done where the sheep gets to live. The first area we discussed is wool and leather – a sheep's covering. Spiritually, this is not a shepherd's covering of the sheep; this is the act of sheep covering other sheep in love and prayer. Notice I said covering and not cover up. As a fellow sheep, I should be able to cover my brother or sister in prayer and love them enough to keep them covered while they are dealing with the issues in their lives. My purpose is not to expose, degrade, or bring them down: it's to show the love of God towards them and help them as much as I can. Every sheep should have the anointing to pray for each other and see the results of their prayers. We should never try and cover up each other's sin. Our purpose should be to support one another as much as possible and assist each other in such a way that causes us both to be successful. There should be such a unity and strength between us that no enemy can penetrate, conquer or destroy.

Although wool and leather are used for similar things such as shoes, clothing, etc., they are two very different products. Wool is the hair of the sheep and leather is made from the skin of the sheep - a double covering, spiritually and physically. Our brothers and sisters in Christ should never have to wonder if they are being supported or covered. They should know beyond any doubt that they have been and are being covered. This means backbiting, gossip, slander and any other negativity should not be named among us. We have to be a part of the solution and not the problem!

To cover one another we have to have the ability to be stretched; we can't be uptight, we must be soft and pliable in the hands of the Lord. It takes a heart like the Father's to be able to love and cover one another with no offense. The word speaks to us about love and how it bears all things, hopes all things and never fails. As long as we have the love of the Father ruling in our lives, we will always cover one another, even in hard situations where we may feel wronged by the other individual. Love will cause you to go beyond where you thought you could go and do far more than what you could ever think you could. So, we can look at the sheep's wool and skin as a banner of LOVE! This love is a double covering; it's two-fold - the "warm and fuzzy' kind of love that covers because it's the right thing to do and the spiritual kind of love that will cover no matter what happens. We as sheep need to display both kinds of love.

The next part of the sheep that we discussed is the catgut. When you think about the strings on the tennis racket, they have to be strong in order to be stretched and have the buoyancy to perform under pressure. The tighter they are the better. They have to have the ability to not break when the ball hits them, and to be strong enough to hit the ball back to your opponent with force. This is the inner strength we must have as spiritual sheep. We must be able to "stand" under pressure and bounce back to serve our opponent no matter what they bring to the table. Inner strength will take us to our ultimate destiny. If you have no inner strength, you will not reach your goals or your destiny in Christ. There may be a lot happening on the outside but if your inner man is strong, you will be able to endure whatever you face on the outside.

The word of God tells us that though our outward man perishes our inward man is renewed day by day (2 Corinthians 4:16). What is on the inside will eventually show on the outside. What comes out of you when you are under pressure shows you who you really are on the inside. So, building your inner man through prayer, praise, worship and relationship with the Father is extremely important. Even the Lord himself is more concerned with our inner man than our outward appearance. Man looks at the outer while the Lord looks at our heart! Is your inner man clean, strong and healthy or are you trying to cover up brokenness, retribution and, anger? Man may never see but the Father who is the good Shepherd sees and knows. Allow Him to heal, deliver and make you free so you can walk forward in the order he has set for your life!

Angela D. Oliphant

Chapter 8:
Caring for the Sheep

Sheep need to be sheared at least once a year so they can remain healthy. When they are sheared, there is little to no fight or resistance from the sheep; they stand quietly and are very amicable while the shepherd does his job. They don't try to run away or fight the shearer. If a sheep must be sheared during the cold months the shepherd, knowing the sheep will be affected by the cold, will put the sheep in a shed for a period of time so they can remain warm until their wool starts to grow back.

As this happens in the natural, how much more should this be happening in the spirit? Pastors ought to know when their sheep should be sheared; and it should never be a process that is abusive or painful. If the shepherd sees that the sheep will be affected by the environment they are in, it is up to the shepherd to take them to a safe place for shearing and keep them there until they are prepared to weather the environment again. Not every sheep is the same and it's the responsibility of the shepherd to know the sheep he or she is caring for. In nature, sheep are animals of prey; their systems have adapted to hide any obvious signs of illness to prevent being targeted by predators. So, it is the duty of the shepherd to know when the sheep are sick. They should see the signs and address them accordingly, instead of waiting for the sheep to tell them what is going on or until the sickness has overtaken the sheep before they try and do something.

Three distinctive ways a shepherd will know that the sheep is ill are:

1. The sheep is eating very little.
2. The sheep is talking (vocalizing) excessively.
3. The sheep lack energy or spirit.

Two ways to prevent this are good nutrition and reducing stress. Pastors need to make sure that the "meal" they are serving the sheep is well-balanced and nutritional. This meal must meet the needs of all who sit at their table on a Sunday morning or even during the week at Bible Study. Each sheep must walk away with something of value to their relationship and walk with God. No sheep should leave empty and unfulfilled. A good shepherd/pastor will take the time needed in the presence of the Lord to make sure the meal they prepare is just what each sheep needs.

Shepherds should also take authority over the atmosphere in which their sheep reside, causing their ambience to be one of peace and tranquility. They don't want to see their sheep stressed and uneasy, afraid or on edge because of what's around them. If they want powerful, productive sheep, they must not be stressed out. Even in the natural, if sheep get anxious, their bodies release hormones that cause post-slaughter meat to spoil quickly due to a higher growth of bacteria. This happens mainly when the sheep is fearful or in pain but it can also happen when the sheep are in transition or being handled. Low stress handling is essential in managing sheep. It is up to the shepherd to handle their charges with the utmost care and to help transition them in the best way possible. To get the best from the sheep they must be given the best care possible.

Unfortunately, we have it all backwards in today's churches. You have the sheep taking care of the shepherd, making sure he is not stressed but surrounded by an environment of peace. I'm not saying we shouldn't honor those whom God has placed in authority over us. We absolutely should; however, a true Shepherd covers his sheep and gives extra care, if you will, to those sheep that have been pulled away from the flock and are being groomed to begin to give milk – in the spiritual, those who have been set apart for specific training. At times, some sheep are pulled away in a process called tethering because the milking sheep can't be with all the other sheep. What would happen if Shepherds began to take care of the sheep in the same way as a physical shepherd cared for his natural sheep? How many church buildings would be filled to overflowing if the sheep were shown the unconditional love they needed? If the sheep could enter into a place where they felt safe, loved, at peace – a true shelter from all the storms in their lives? Think about it.

What an awesome experience for a sheep to know that they are supported and loved by those whom God has set over them. Sheep who are loved and supported will always give that love and support to the shepherd.

Angela D. Oliphant

Conclusion

When God created the earth and us in it, he also created order. Everything had purpose: take the Bible, for example. Not one word was written haphazardly or just for the "fun" or it. Every word, every life story, every parable was written with purpose and order in mind. However, when purpose is not known and order is not followed, chaos follows and things that need to be accomplished will be unfinished and unaccomplished.

The word says that in the beginning, the world was without form and void, even as the Holy Ghost hovered over the face of the waters (Genesis 1:1-2). Then something great happened! God spoke and what he said brought forth change. All the elements were already there to bring about something great but until he spoke order into them, they didn't know how to shine forth in all their greatness and glory.

This is why I praise God today and forever. Because I serve a speaking God: he is not a statue, he's not a picture on a billboard, nor an animal, fish, food or a piece of furniture! He is a living, breathing, moving and speaking God! Hallelujah! And in order to move forward and receive the blessing upon our lives we must allow God to speak to us and bring forth our full potential, allowing us to become what we have been designed to be. We can no longer be formless and void.

When we look at things in the word of God like the Tabernacle, we see how daunting the task to create it was (Exodus 26). The plans were very detailed and God had to speak forth how to put it all together. He showed how it should be built, what items should be put in the tabernacle upon completion; he even told them what kind of wood to use, what materials to utilize (gold, silver, brass, or wood), and what colors, size, length, height and width everything should be.

The Father was not only meticulous about the tabernacle but also those who built it: the craftsmen were not chosen because of their skill and ability, but because of their willing spirit. Likewise, those who served in the tabernacle were chosen because of their hearts. And regardless of whether they were a porter or a priest, God gave intricate instructions that were to be adhered to.

This is why I started studying the sheep: if the Father compares us to sheep, I want to know what a sheep does, how it lives, how it interacts with its surroundings, etc. He could have compared us to any other animal in the world but he specifically said sheep. There is significance to everything the Father does. He has a design and a plan that must be followed in order for us to prosper and move forward! Take the time to really study and see what the Father has in store for you. When you look at the human body and all the different parts, you'll see that regardless of significance, each part serves a purpose and in order for the body to function correctly it needs all of its parts. In the Old Testament, it was the physical tabernacle; in the New Testament, the word of God says we are now that tabernacle. This speaks volumes to me: to say we are the tabernacle means God has specific plans for us, plans he has designed for us.

Everyone was created as an original and we are all uniquely designed. When we all come *together* and work *together*, we become a beautiful picture that the Father intended. However, if we aren't secure in whom we are and what we have been designed to do, we will never live our lives to our fullest potential. Most people don't fulfill their purpose because they compare themselves to others and not to their destiny. We should never "size" ourselves up against each other, we need to seek the Father, see what he has set up for us and go strictly by his plan. The God we serve knows why we are here and why he has placed us on the earth; so, seek him until you hear his voice and see what his plan is for you. Don't ever try to duplicate someone else.

The Shepherd, The Sheep and The Sheepdog

Angela D. Oliphant

The Shepherd, The Sheep and The Sheepdog

*Thank you, Father,
for calling our lives to order!*

Angela D. Oliphant

Prophetic Poetic Prayer

My prayer today is for order
Father please order my day,
whisper to me the plan you have for me
the order you have set for today
I sit quietly awaiting to hear your voice
I can't move or be or do if order doesn't rule my day
Please take all the chaotic pieces of my yesterday
and mold them and make them be the ladder into
my order of today
My footsteps you order
My mind you order
My heart you order
My life
Every intricate fiber of who I am order and
please make it right when I open my eyes and
seek your face in the solitude of the morning
your plan and order
floods my heart with joy and excitement
for the order of today
As the night gives way to the light of day
and birds began to sing and

Angela D. Oliphant

the crisp wind blows saying thank you
for the order of today
No more scattered
No more confusion
No more self-doubt and hate
because I look in the face of order
I can celebrate my life today
No hope deferred No heart sick
No broken pieces in disarray
Just the rhythmic pattern of a song called order
that is transforming my life today
Order, pattern, rhythm and flow
systematic plan order
flowing from the Father's heart now seen,
embraced and desired a path
that was once covered now is ready to be traveled
Order
Order
Order
Order
This is the Father's Master plan
A life filled with order
A life of success
A life directed by His hand

The Shepherd, The Sheep and The Sheepdog

Angela D. Oliphant

About the Author

Angela D. Oliphant is at heart a teacher. She grew up in the small town of Aiken, South Carolina and she always had dreams that took her further than the boundaries where she physically lived.

Angela has always had a love for words because through them she saw and experienced life in a whole new light. Early in her life, she realized words could transform, train and equip every person who would take the time to read and embrace them - whether through books, magazines, or even a newspaper. With this passion and thirst to help others understand the wealth found in words, she has set out on a mission to teach, train and equip all who will listen and apply words to their lives that will bring order in the midst of chaos and a calm in the midst of any storm. She believes that the right words spoken at the right time in the lives of others can elevate their thinking to the place where there are no limitations or boundaries to what they want to accomplish in their lives.

Through poetry, short stories, articles, and public speaking – she has presented opportunities that will bring a positive change to the lives of all who will listen and understand that their entire world can literally be transformed- "One Word at a Time."

www.ingramcontent.com/pod-product-compliance
Lightning Source LLC
Chambersburg PA
CBHW071505070526
44578CB00001B/449